A Tree Never Leaves Before the Snow Falls

Lumijnfroost

A Tree Never Leaves
Before the Snow Falls

Poetry from the Half-Life

Peer Lumijnfroost

Twaanévie Publishing House
Blacksburg, Virginia

Opèlaan Ïnktûr, an imprint of Twaanévie Publishing House
845 Deercroft Drive
Blacksburg, Virginia 24060
www.twaaneviepublishinghouse.com

Publisher's Note: This is a work of fiction. Names, characters, places, and incidents are a product of the author's imagination. Locales and public names are sometimes used for atmospheric purposes. Any resemblance to actual people, living or dead, or to businesses, companies, events, institutions, or locales is completely coincidental.

Ordering Information:
Additional copies may be ordered at Amazon.com

Queries and/or Quantity Purchase Discounts:
Contact the Publisher at twaaneviepublishinghouse@gmail.com.

Lumijnfroost: A Tree Never Leaves before the Snow Falls/ Peer Lumijnfroost.
-- 1st ed.
ISBN 978-0-9660055-7-8
Library of Congress Control Number: 2017900150

Printed in the United States of America

Fáilte

To those of us
who hesitate and ruminate,
equivocate and vacillate,
who gravitate
in secrecy
to whimsy flight and fantasy,
bluesy speak and poetry,
debauchery and revelry,
and all things seen invisibly;
who dream at noon
that love strikes soon
and carries them from drudgery.
To those of us
who agitate and levitate
let Life and Love cohabitate
these pages cool and amorous.

Note to the Reader

This collection of poems is a companion to the book Life in the Half-Life *in which Peer shares his experience, first as a young apprentice in Florence in 1498, then to his introduction to the Realm Dimidium (the Half-Life) in 1501, and his journey since then as he has observed the Realm Modicum (ordinary life) from the unfiltered perspective of the parallel Half-Life. Over the past five centuries he has met a number of significant historical figures while pushing against the darkness of the times—foremost slavery, prejudice, war, inquisitions, religious intolerance, poverty, inequality, and ignorance. On rare occasions, he has returned to the Realm Modicum for brief periods but is inevitably pulled back into the land of magic, where the world has never been a 'bubble off plumb.'*

The majority of the author's work was written in Peer's native language, il Toscano, although certain sections were written in the vernacular where he lived at that particular time, including Latin, Dutch, French, early modern English, Gaelic (Irish), and German, among others. Over the past five years Mr Lumijnfroost has translated his original text into modern English so that his work may be presented to a wider audience.

The author wishes to clarify that any errors or loss in translation are the sole responsibility of the author, and he takes full credit for them.

-trp, publisher, Blacksburg.

Earth, a hornet's nest
hanging in the midnight sky.
In this drop of liquid ink,
billions swarming mad.

–PEER LUMIJNFROOST

Contents

A Tree Never Leaves Before the Snow Falls

1 Aoibhneas

(EEV-NASS)

A sense of bliss or delight;
a complete filling of our senses

London, England.
18 Oct 1979.

Eavesdrop

letters gather together
in parliament beneath
her swollen rain gutter
outside a London mews.
Lovers in muffled tones
voice what the young heart wills.
Two vowels joined to love;
three single words, one breath.
Eye love ewe, he tells her.
I love you back, she says.
Words cuddled together.
It is well past nightfall;
the Queen is fast asleep
before the two emerge
from the sheltered shadows
and amble arm-in-arm
to the warmth of the pub.

Het koffiehuis, Amsterdam.
14 Feb 1680.

from blossom and bean
to cherries and chocolate
fresh love in between

Charleston Harbour. The New World.
21 Dec 1815.

sweet melancholy
dark fruit amongst the brambles
free for the taking

Park on Via di Capaccio, Florence.
6 May 1498.

Old Flame

wax of the candle
future memories
of whispered longings
illicit cuddles
wandering passions
released and guarded
by a well-placed flame

Essex, England.
20 Jun 1917.

Féileacán

It is
better for the butterfly
that the sun shines
here
where the rain will wait
to fall another day

so little time
for these restless souls
to flit and flutter
before the moon moves over
and quiescence sets in
between blades of grass
or under a leaf

for me,
I relish the rain,
the thunder and bright bolts—
the clash of Earth
and Universe
in the upper blue rim
that holds the dark at bay
while summer souls
carry on their flighty ways.

Central Park. New York City.
17 Mar 1998.

Parsippany

I have no idea what it means,
but I like the sound of it.
I can imagine the old man
sitting on his stool
in the ivory tower
peering over
his incomplete dictionary,
dipping his pen
in the inkwell,
while running his other hand
through his beard,
grizzled and brought together
with a blue bow a foot
south of his chin.

I imagine he's wearing gold
pantaloons and lime-coloured
slippers with curled-up toes,
and a pirate's white puffy shirt.
Yes, I can see him now
as he is just finishing
the 'y' of Parsippany.

There is a slight pause,
perceptible only in a blink,
as his hand awaits the electronic
signal from his brain
telling him the precise definition.

He assumes it will be an adjective,
but who knows, perhaps a noun—
a common noun,
maybe a proper noun,
like a town
where the persnickety
and the pedantic
take residence in houses
where the front doors
are conveniently located in the back.
Perhaps,
but then only the old man
really knows for sure,
and he's not yet spoken.

Colchester Castle, Colchester, England.
21 Feb 1872.

Once, I was Adam

When I was twelve
I had a dream
that I was the only
man left on Earth.
There were no cities,
roads, or houses.
No cages of any kind.
The animals were free
to roam, to fly, to swim.
I was the new Adam
before the second Eve
had time to arrive.
God was with me,
of course.
We walked through
herds of gentle deer
parting before us
like the Red Sea.
He told me I needed
to relax and let go
of a world that wouldn't
last beyond his version
of tomorrow. By morning,
my dream was a thousand
years away from me, a distant
and foreign presence.

Il Panifico bakery, Florence.
7 Jun 1501.

Wishing

At the top end
of the cold world
a boy pulls a
penny from his
pocket and looks
at the old year.
As he had watched
the others do,
he closes his eyes,
makes a wild wish,
and then tosses
the copper coin
into the dark.
It is gone, now
beyond his reach.
He holds the rail
and leans far down,
straining to hear
the tell-tale sound
of his one true
wish now confirmed.

2 Suaimhneas

(SOO-IV-NASS)

Serenity.

Llanfachraeth, Wales.
24 Mar 1699.

short-term memory
just living in the moment
life of the goldfish

Edinburgh, Scotland.
20 Oct 1959.

through the magic of sleep
I am six feet
trim and chiselled
dark-haired and intact
a content accountant
prolific poet
playful husband
accessible father
I can play the banjo
harmonica and piano
I am fluent in Irish
German and French
I can energise a dying room
a tired story a frayed friend
I can get the gone back
and the going to stay
Through the magic of sleep
in a single word
I am somebody

Caisleán sa Garrán. County Offaly, Ireland.
01 Jan 2000.

Innocence

Dark before the Renaissance
I knew naked innocence
I drank mother's milk
until I could walk
I lay there cold and nude
near my dear mother's breast
a cry's sharp tongue from food
maternal love and rest

In the garden. Florence.
Dusk. 12 Sep 1501.

black is the night
that hides the blue sky
pink is the crush of dawn
the lips of Orabella
the girl my heart is set upon

Voyage across the Atlantic
31 Aug – 02 Oct 1754.

Spoonful of Solitude

I rest in(side
a teaspoon
where
the smooth curve
of its belly
holds me nicely,
keeps me safe
inside the vim
and vigour of
its oval rim.

I imagine
life before
the silver dips
below the murky
water of the
China sea,
while the tea
still broods
in the hollow
skull of the
porcelain pot.

I crave
the honey that
rounds the spoon,
that leaves no
space between
its sweetness and
the outer world,
its amber memory
of flowered Spring
and summer yield.

I feel
the heated
mist that wets
the spoon
before it slips
beneath the
fluid silence,
the oolong
afternoon
of solace
I give myself.

Amsterdam.
02 Apr 1680.

Evensong

A tree never leaves
its appointed spot,
whether the land be
forest, field, or stream;
graveyard or back yard;
kerb side or seaside.
Anchored throughout time,
it lives a backdrop
life, an observer
to the world around.
It harbours the birds,
houses the squirrels,
indulges the boy
who enjoys the climb.
A silent witness
in rough elements,
a reassurance
to us who must live
among creatures far
less dependable.
God bless the stoic
tree that bears us fruit
in shades of shadows
and gives us solace
with the stature of
enveloping grace.

Village de Giverny, France.
14 Jun 1889.

Monet's Palette

Mid morning
garden grace notes
brush of Monet
chrome yellow
madder red
cobalt blue
viridian
green parasol
living smudges
à la Renoir
smidge of whimsy
erratic flight
picture perfect
sight without sound
rapid pivots
the gypsy life
wings for the souls
from dear bodies
now departed
a summer fling
before heading
Home

Mongewell Village, Oxfordshire, England.
21 Apr 1967.

Grim's Ditch

I walk alone along Grim's Ditch.
At this point it is a narrow droveway
near Mongewell and the River Thames.
A nave through the forest, with aisles
of bluebells on either side, it is Monet's
font of inspiration and a poet's treasure.
Here, I am a century or two from London
and the global turmoil we call Life—
atomic bombs, Iron Curtain, Viet Nam.
Yes, when I am here in the forest,
I am never far from Shakespeare
and the characters he brought to life
whether in truth or wicked imagination.
Here, I am me, myself, and I.
Mortal body, mind, and soul.
Mortarium, pistillum, anima.
Bones and logic aside, the essence prevails.
What was not yet clear in kindergarten,
or the roller-coaster days of puberty
or the moans and groans of middle life
is now firmly installed as truth in my mind:
We are mortally bound to the past,
securely tethered to the written word
left behind by those reduced to dust,
just as I am lifted here by a Ditch formed
by hands callused back in the Bronze Age.

Pike County, Kentucky.
11 Jun 1823.

In Fields Unclothed

In the morning of our mind
we walk the fields unclothed.
The worldview is fresh, green—
animal and mineral
and tons of vegetable,
not financial, provincial
or even the slightest political.
Truth then is as simple
as love, kindness, and peace.
These fields have no edge
or hedge to hem them in,
and we have no pockets
to line our treasure.

3 Sceitimíní

(SKETCH-A-MEENY)

Bubbling joy.

Paris, France.
11 May 1789.

storm the castle
raise the roof
bore the barrel
it's a hundred proof!

Park on Via di Capaccio, Florence.
6 May 1498.

en garde
I planted
the sword
in the sheath.
prise de fer
parry, thrust
forward cross
glide and lunge
engagement
until the door
flew open
and blew
an ill wind
that burned
cheeks red
and left
balls blue.

River Arno, Outside Florence.
14 Sep 1501.

the dry earth trembles
when the stallion mounts the mare,
dust clouds rise en masse

London Docks.
Night before my departure to America.
30 Aug 1754.

Sylvan Fun

Naked we enter
the forest that catches rain
in shallow green cups

playful we shatter
a mirror of the blue sky
the cold liquid sky

earnest we ladder
the height of a mighty oak
on wings of wet feet

enthralled we scatter
the images of summer
naked as jay birds

On the outskirts of Memphis, Tennessee.
In a cornfield where the crows fly.
27 Aug 1998.

One Mississippi

In a field at night
he mounts his lover
so assertively
the way that she likes.
Then once inside, he

whispers sweet somethings
into waiting ears
before he begins
his deep, thrusting moves.
He is primed for love—

perhaps a bit too
much for his own good.
He worries that he
might reach nirvana
sooner than his love.

He counts in German—
a WASP-ish fallback—
eins. zwei. drei. vier. fünf.
sechs—he stops at sex.
Begins then to think

of other things; now
finds himself aboard
a German U-boat.
It's quiet, dead-still.
The enemy waits

on the surface
but down below he
is hot and sweaty.
He shifts his weight
while she counts the stars.

When she strokes his cheek,
he pushes forward
and plies again the
open sea, where winds
whisper sweet somethings

in his lover's ear
as they become one
and rock together
in the open field
of corn, five feet high,

as he counts, this time
in French, the country
of good wine and cheese.
Camembert and Brie—
both so soft and white.

He smiles and she asks
what he is thinking.
Does he tell her he
is counting the times
they have been in this

field before today?
Or that he will soon
recite the Gettysburg
Address in his head,
or Frost—anything

to cleave this rocking
from the quick trigger
located somewhere
in the deep nethers
of his masculine,

horny, mortal frame?
He keeps up his pace
as she waits to hear
that he has thought of
only her since he

first awoke and joined
the rest of the world
in their monkey suits.
He prefers birthday suits.
Does he tell her that?

He suspects she knows,
but he cannot tell
her his usual
jokes; not this moment.
He says "I love you"

instead. It's a safe
answer where they are.
She responds as he
hoped and clasps her arms
tight around his neck.

One Mississippi.
He counts to thirty
in a measured pace.
One Alabama.
He shifts position,

solving equations
as he presses on.
Y equals three-X;
X equals twenty.
Y equals sixty.

X cubed equals eight,
so X equals two,
too good to be true,
he tells himself
Again and again.

"I love you back," she
says before a kiss,
a kiss that deepens.
His body responds...
A. E. I. O. U.

Syncopated vowels
packed with manly force.
The train's approaching
the station; he feels it
coming. Mercury

is rising faster
than he can handle.
He wants to hold back,
to keep on going.
But he's past the point.

There's no way to stop.
He wants to but can't.
His heart is racing
faster than before.
The pressure pushes him.

He screams his lover's
name in a volume
that scatters the crows
and leaves his Venus
in both shock and awe.

A TREE NEVER LEAVES BEFORE THE SNOW FALLS

Göthe University library. Frankfurt.
16 Oct 2011.

behind blue shutters
butterflies brush the stomach
love waits for the night

beneath the teddy
the sweetest smell of jasmine
the bare skin unknown

before blue shutters
butterflies fan her tulips
my heart aches for night

Grafton House, Isleworth, England.
12 May 1751.

A Lawn the Lake

Silly loon and lily swan
swim beside the manicured lawn.
Now picture me upon the grass
copping a feel and getting some ass.

There's more to life than sheltered beds,
shuttered glass, and jelly spreads.
There's war to the east, famine in the south.
The sanity of the world has bottomed out.

Black is black and blue is blue;
the future wants to link the two.
Yesterday came and left us red;
'better left in debt than dead.'

Or perhaps I've gotten the saying wrong.
I often use words that don't belong.
But then I'm the chap who has the chance
to see the birds without his pants.

Onward and upward!

4 Caoineadh

(KEEN-ACH)

Laments.

Florence.
9 Apr 1982.

a drop from God's eye
contains the quick and the dead
racing between trees

On the Iceberg, North Atlantic.
17 Apr 1912.

RMS Titanic

Living the moment
cocktails, caviar, champagne
dancing through musical sheets
unnoticed in the laughter
a scrape of hard ice
the tilt of danger
glass breaks, lights flicker
cracks in the dance floor
Life frozen in time
remnants tossed aside
the fine bone china at rest
beneath wet blankets
at the bottom of the sea

Park on Via di Capaccio, Florence.
6 Aug 1501.

three hearts two genders
one union of two centres
second man out cold

Amsterdam.
16 May 1695.

Birdcage Blues

I live in a birdcage
of my own choosing.
I built it myself,
this sad contraption,
and climbed in a long
time ago, when I knew
nothing of the world
and even less of me.

Wings, I have learned,
are utterly useless
inside a cage.
They have no place they
can carry you and are
completely unfit
to lift the drop door
that could set you free

Early Evening, Amsterdam.
14 Nov 1679.

flowing beneath ice
the stream never stops to catch
hungry schools of fish

Oesling, Luxembourg.
3 Mar 1988.

Kite at Night

If I could fly a kite at night,
I would most certainly do it.
I would hang a paper lantern—
in all likelihood a green one—
from its diamond-framed cross beam
and let the half-moon hoist it up.
It would be my star in the sky
that I could pull and tug at will;
one thing I could control before
falling asleep and letting go.

Accademia di Contabilità, Florence.
20th Aug 1501.

Coram Deo

We live in the 'some time later,'
on the outskirts of eternity.
Immersed in the body,
confined to the elements,
time-boxed to unknown seconds,
and bothered by an inkling,
placed in us at birth,
that a great source, shrouded
in clarity, always surrounds us.
Omniscient and omnipotent.
He moves to our movements,
filling in the space we leave.
Always in sync to our breath.
He holds the life in our hands
until that singular moment,
inevitable but anxiously awaited,
when we are then absent of body,
iterum in the presence of God.

The East End, London.
12 Mar 1969.

Chalk Dust

In a tray
there is a pile
of coloured dust
Flakes of chalk,
spittle of the teacher's
talk

I am a boy
inside my heart
I watch the ashes fall
from the orange stick
in her hand
and gather on the tray
as sands of time
without the glass

She talks to the wall,
a deaf plane and mute
as well, poor soul.
She cannot see the faces
that look so blank.

She underlines in red
to emphasise
what she has said
and peppers the blackboard
with stars of blue and green

At the end of the day
the books are closed
and shades are drawn.
Chairs are raised
and erasers clapped
and along the tray
remains the dust—
numbers and letters,
symbols and fractions
broken down
and jumbled up
amongst the graves
of the fallen stars

Copenhagen, Denmark.
13 Mar 1990.

Cobblestones

Sometimes when I sleep
I see piles of shoes
stacked like cobblestones—
remnants of the past.
Plain and simple shoes,
boxy, non-descript.
Nothing in high heels
or high-top sneakers;
No fancy buckles
or glitter laces;
Nike or Gucci,
not a Prada.
Worn by simple folk,
they are practical,
chunky with worn soles.
They are black, dark brown,
or white with grey scuffs.
On some, the laces
hide inside the heel,
others tied in knots
or the perfect bow—
bows double-knotted
for the little ones.
Some joined to their mates
like genetic strands
of man and woman,

tied together, one
from each of the two.
Too many eyelets
have no lace at all.
Those shoes are naked;
their tongue and quarters
wide open, exposed
to the elements

I am now haunted
by the pile of shoes,
chimneys and showers
and all things not said
within earshot of
polite company.
Haunted forever
by the cobblestones
that once held the soles
of those taken too soon
from a world so lost.

Halifax, Nova Scotia.
29 Apr 1912.

Night Orphans

The whales swam north
toward the Arctic
Sea while I slept.
I tossed and turned
while they pushed for
icy waters.
I snored and I
snuggled in warmth
and childhood dreams.
Pinocchio
was in my head.
I imagine
inside every
whale Geppetto
stands on his boat
with Figaro
calling his boy.
Whale after whale,
boat after boat,
fathers cry out
for their lost sons.
The cries jolt me
wide awake.
Clammy and cold,
I am marooned
on a small raft;

All I can see
are the thousand
stars without names.
'The Night Orphans,'
my muse calls them.
I pick one out;
a faint green light.
I give him my
name—Lumijnfroost.
Cold Light. But I
know he will watch
the whales until
they are back home.
And with that thought
I finally
fall fast to sleep.

PEER LUMIJNFROOST

Blacksburg, Virginia.
04 Nov 2016.

telling the bees

Someone has to tell them,
so it might as well be you.
I mean, it can't be me;
I've been afraid of bees
ever since they flew
up my pant leg while
I waited to build a barn.
The pain re-visits me
at night sometimes when
I'm restless and can't sleep.
Bees never sleep, or so
I've heard; they're too
busy putting away their
honey and tucking in
the little ones, the future
of their thriving hive.

I've never been good
at delivering bad news;
it's not in my nature.
I cry too easily; I wear
too many sad stories
on my sleeve, especially
when I halt to remember
the swarm that turned
my young boy's thigh
into a rosy pin cushion.

But someone must tell them;
it is an obligation we accepted
when Adam left the garden
with the queen in his palm.
They do the heavy lifting
to give us fruit and honey
and all they ask in return
is important news from time
to time. A pending marriage,
the bundle in the baby carriage,
the passing of the beekeeper.

Someone should tell them
that global warming is real.
If no one else, at least
they should know the truth.
We owe them as much.

Just knock gently on the hive,
most gently, mind you,
whisper the news in a voice
low enough to be heard,
bow twice and then depart,
leaving a sweet something
for all of them to share.

It is a simple thing to do,
as I say, but I'm not the one
to do it. It's just not in me.

Hastings, England.
17 Jul 1963.

Rock, Scissors, Paper

Granted,
granite is the hardest,
shears and scissors
the sharpest,
but paper cuts
are murder.

A rock may tap
a window,
and scissors cut
the cord,
but paper holds
the cards.

Reading, England.
9 Aug 1978.

Omnia Solus

and when his life is over
he will be no different
than the brittle black fly
now
stuck in the nook of the sill

5 Draíocht

(DREE-oct)

that which is unseen.

Huis van Engelbrecht, Amsterdam.
24 Dec 1679.

even the devil
feels the light snowfall
leagues above his head

Wiltshire, England.
15 Sep 1961.
Observing the ancient spirits at work.

the blue ghosts of Stonehenge
reflect the bluestone gravestones
well-worn and held happenstance
in the shadows of the giant Sarsens
Modern minds scratch their heads
trying to understand what it all means—
the stone Pi's, fallen altar, buried heel—
while these ghosts who know the secret
amble without rush or purpose
within the muted space we call prehistoric

Grafton House, Isleworth. England.
4 Jun 1907.

Quiet solitude
marks the evening repast
in dreams, fine spirits

Wiltshire, England.
15 Sep 1961.

inside the teapot
the steam caresses the walls
dark water delights

Bath, England.
24 Dec 1993.

in Deo manet

the mist is a precursor
to the blue sky far beyond
our grasp if we choose to reach
not
on our own but with God's help.

London, England.
11 Apr 1977.

smiles frozen in time
Kodachrome in a dark room
spirits on paper

Nicholas' House. Florence.
21 Sep 1501.

1.19 am

the clock in the hall
pushes time forward
as the dust settles
in
the creaks of the stairs
that betray the steps
of the Half-Lifer
who
wanders like a ghost
caught between the worlds
of Heaven and Earth

La vechhia cantina (the Wine Cellar), Florence.
14 Sep 1501. Near Midnight.

Kairos

In the beginning
Kairos walked the Earth
and sat with Adam
and Eve in the cool
of the garden day.
Long before the fig,
they delighted Him.
Long before the snake,
the pomegranate,
and the taste of sin
pushed Him out of sight,
He called them by name

Farleigh Hungerford Castle, near Bath, England.
11 Nov 1746.

Ghosts and Phantoms

Ghosts are nothing to fear—
the translucent ones, that is.
They inhabit physical space,
lower the temperature of the room,
and moan when your courage is low.
They give a home a certain mystique
and graveyards a certain gravitas.
But that is all they really do.
They carry little weight and have lost
all perspective of a normal life.
They are sad commentaries
of lives mis-spent and unfulfilled.

Now, let's talk about the other ghosts—
the ones that live in the mind
and never leave despite the pleading,
ranting and raving, and cajoling.
They are a menace to normalcy,
and any real chance of happiness.
While a man can give up
but a single ghost, he can father
a thousand phantoms to plague
his sleep and worry his poor wife.

Phantoms soon morph into dark
daemons that do battle with you day
and night, Monday to Sunday.
There is no romanticism in them;
they exist merely to bring you down
to a level you would not recognize
in those rare moments of clarity
between infancy and dementia.

Near Lake Geneva. Duchy of Savoy.
1 Jun 1519.

Vibrations of the Four Strings

L'espace entre la naissance
et la mort est lumière du jour
espace blanc entre les lignes
le vrai personnel de vie
que soulève le sombre notes
les vibrations des quatre cordes
Grace. Dieu. Amour. Espoir.

the space between birth
and death is daylight
white space between lines
the true staff of life
that holds the dark notes
vibrations of four
God. Dust. Air. Essence.

6 baile

(BAL-YEH)

town, home, village;
a sense of place.

Turin. Duchy of Savoy.
13 Jan 1514.

missals in the pews
angels in the rafters
sinners at the door
God is everywhere

Château Amboise, France. Leonardo's gravesite.
2 May 1719.

Invisible Trinity

Faith in the unknown
Hope in a life born again
Love for each other

Leonardo's Apartment. Early Eve. Florence.
14 Sep 1501.

behind every door
you find anxious people pray
before every knock

Ulmenstraße. Frankfurt am Main. Deutschland.
16 Oct 2001.

doors and windows

We slay the tree
to bear the door
We set it free
on hinge shut tight
Solid, secure
we sleep at night

We burn the sand
to liquid glass
Bubble on pipe
we blow it flat
to window panes
we then prop up

to let in light
fine coloured stars
and views of things
still wild and free
we leave outdoors
with bolt and key

Grafton House. Isleworth. England.
A warm Spring day.
28 Apr 1751.

Bees on Break

Bees line the shore
of the bird bath
like Guernsey's heavy with milk.
I try to imagine their little
lips lapping the fresh water
on their short, five minute break.
I can hear the murmurs
of gossip out of the sides
of their mouths.

O, the things they must see
as they flit from flower
to flower, one yard
to the next.
Who knows better about
the birds and the bees
and all things private
than the butler, the bar-maid,
and the busy honeybee?

Kilkenny, Ireland.
10 May 1603.

Éire

One isle, two churches
two men, one mission
one stem, three clovers
three crosses, one Christ
one land, two people
two shackles, one chain
one fort, four towers
four kingdoms, one lord
one life, two fathers
two flocks, one shepherd
one divide, One love.

Leonardo's Apartment. Early Eve. Florence.
14 Sep 1501.

the creaks in the stairs
betray the spirits
inside this very house

Lancaster, Pennsylvania.
6 May 1998.

Only in Pennsylvania

Only in Pennsylvania
could you have towns
of polar opposites—
Virginville and Intercourse,
Blue Ball and Paradise—
quartered in the same county.
Bareville and Johnsonville,
Hop Bottom and Bath,
then Bedford and Pillow,
Mount Pleasant and the ultimate
Mount Joy over Good Intent.
But let us not focus too much
on the lusty and the carnal.
There's also Weedville and Stonerstown,
Cokeville, Scotch Hill, and Brandywine.
There's Wawa beyond the Dry Tavern,
leading to Hellertown and Hecktown.
If Mars and Apollo are too lofty,
I prefer Slickville and Slippery Rock,
over Shickskinny and Shinglehouse.
Live Easy is preferable to Grindstone.
Topton better than Tipton.
Prosperity and Progress and Cashtown
over Factoryville and Effort.
And, if Cracker Jack is not enough,
there's always Sugarcreek, Flourtown,
and Bakerstown before Krumsville.

Which one to choose—
Glassport or Rockhill?
Pennville or Inkerman?
Or, back again, to Hosensack,
which sounds strangely similar
to the German word for the most
sensitive part of the male anatomy.
And somewhere in the nethers
of my earthy and sotted mind
I see the road sign for Tuckerton
and wonder how long it took
for the local boys to modify
what the town fathers had so
proudly and firmly erected.

In a forest outside Oxford. England.
9 Apr 1597.

Nightlife

The creatures
nocturnal
need the mask
of night to
pass the time
when moonlight
reigns above
the foxes
and the owl,
bat and mole
and all that
breathe to howl.
They stalk from
pitch to black,
hang about,
until they
catch their kill.
Then they race
the old moon
home again,
fade to black,
forever
held to live
where the sun
dare not shine

Normandy. France.
6 Jun 1744.

A Rise to Rest

Beyond the shores of the moment
there is a rise of flowered grass,
flecks of colour jostling each
other in the Norman breeze.
It draws me to its ample spot,
so I walk its narrow path to rest.
I am long spent from a life of stress.
From here, I see the wide ocean,
shades of slate beneath the blue sky.
Always a blue sky, never grey,
Blue is the true colour of hope,
reflections of natural light;
grey, the reality of life,
the sure mortality of here.

Brighton, England.
01 Oct 1872.

Tucker

Tucker puts his front
paws on the side
of the rocking chair
and stares out the window.
He is focused
on the curved driveway
and the pending arrival
of his trusted best friend.
Oh, if life could just be
that pure and simple
for the rest of us.
Imagine how we'd live.

New Mexico, United States.
11 Jun 1999.

Shiprock

In the distance
        she appears a massive ship,
leaning to port,
        her sails expectant with air.
She is alone,
        all around a desert sea,
racing onward
        to reach Four Corners by dusk.

Whitstable, Kent, England.
01 Aug 1973.

On Marlborough Street

I was sitting at the kerb
waiting for the ice cream van
I knew would never come.
I was avoiding work again,
wishing I could be anywhere else.
When along came a flock of geese.
It didn't take much effort
to join them. I just stood up
and in a blink or two I was
there among them, on the edge of the Vee.
We flew South toward the village.
I spied the East Coast track
that bends around the mountain
and the two quarries by my house.
What a grand view I had. The bird's eye.
It all looked so peaceful and simple.
A distant place from the nine to five.
I found myself forgetting to breathe.
Life is not so much a box of chocolates
as it is a model train set in circular motion.
And the flock that flies South will, I know,
in time turn around and fly back over
my workplace to drop me off. In the meantime,
though, I will leave my shoes on the ground,
my hands in the air, and my head in the clouds.

7 Comhluadar

(CO-LOO-DER)

the enjoyable company of friends.

Frankfurt am Main.
16 Oct 2001.

Pohénégamook

Every now and then you run
across a place that is a cross
between a cuss and an incantation.
Abracadabra! Alakazam!
Opportunities come but once
and, at a hundred and ten
kilometres an hour,
they pass in a beat of an eye.

Göthe University library. Frankfurt.
16 Oct 2011.

paradise in space
a God-size pebble
pitted and filled with water
spins circles around the flame
as we live under white clouds
lined with black bellies
thunder and lightning
as we run pell-mell
seeking dry cover

Mount Vernon, Virginia.
16 Dec 1799.
Two days after Washington's death.

The Man of Colour

I was disappointed
the first time I met
a man of colour.
I had heard wild stories
how they would upend
the white world we lived,
destroying completely
centuries of sameness,
denigrating our
treasured Mother English,
blemishing the white
lilies of the field,
wholly Anglo Saxon.
Yes, the day I met
him and shook his hand,
I was disappointed
the man of colour
was not blue or shade
of green but was in fact
not so very much
different than me.

Charlotte, North Carolina.
12 Nov 1999.

They, You, We

They sit on busses and park benches;
they dress the kerbs with ragged colour
and break the serenity of our comfort.
They hold the blank faces of the hard life,
the numbness of their trips and falls.
They look on us with pitiful eyes
and speak to us in the drawn-out
drawls of a long and disconnected story.

You like the straight lines and wait
for the white man to tell you to walk.
You keep your hands in your pocket
and fiddle to count the exact change.
You err always on the side of caution
and steer clear of the ragged colours.
You polish your shoes and manoeuvre
past the oval puddles of cloudy brown.
You fly kites with your kids and wish
the green benches were open to sit.
You wonder why they linger and clutter,
with nothing to do, no purpose at all.
You wish they would just disappear
overnight.

We wake and wonder what the world
will leave next on our doorstep.
We think inwardly and live within
the perfect circles we have drawn.
We let into the hive the bees we know,
wasting little time on They and You.

Shakespeare's Forest, outside Oxford.
10 Apr 1597.

The Spirits of Shakespeare

I sleep in the moonshade
of a giant green oak.
Around me the critters
crawl and roam, fly and hide
inside my private dream.
The spirits of Shakespeare
surround my sleeping flesh.
Puck kicks my naked sole
while Thisbe holds tightly
to the red mulberry.
From out of the bushes
the playwright emerges
to join his characters
pulling me from slumber

Calais, France.
2 Feb 1749.

Renaissance

When I lived in the Renaissance days,
I knew a family who lived on the ocean.
Not on a boat, of course, but on the surface.
Their bare feet walked in puddles all day;
their mobile village of conical and oval
tents was in a perpetual state of sailing
or moving with the maritime currents.
Driftwood for fires, flotsam for supplies;
fish for frying, the whales for ploughing.

Their eldest son David once studied
with Michelangelo, but he tired easily
of the back-breaking work and took up
modelling for Il Divino. Disillusion by
the lack of privacy, he rowed home,
canvass and paints in tow, and created
the scenery wagons that hid the family
so well from the pirates and Portuguese
ships that ventured the virgin Atlantic.

I heard, years later, that they had tired
of the moveable sea and came ashore
on the Irish coast near Ballybunion,
where they live there yet today on the cliffs
with one foot on the sod and one in the air.

8 Aimsir

(AM-SHIR)

time. weather. the seasons.

Caisleán sa Garrán. County Offaly, Ireland.
01 Jan 2000.

millennial moment

the centuries unfold
until the Millennial
moment has arrived
all of life stands still
before the old world
jumps two feet forward
then one step back

Caisleán sa Garrán. County Offaly, Ireland.
14 Sep 1752.

from julian to gregorian

eleven days lost,
vanished in Autumn
like the morning frost.
These poor lost moments—
days, hours, minutes—
skipped and forgotten

A TREE NEVER LEAVES BEFORE THE SNOW FALLS

Huis van Engelbrecht, Amsterdam.
24 Dec 1679.

in sickness and health
two hearts remain connected
even after death

Crossing the Atlantic. Returning home to England.
12 Apr 1861.

ripe cherry on stone
the cardio-arthritis
of two old lovers

Il Panifico bakery. Florence.
14 Sep 1501.

debits and credits
accounting by the numbers
depreciation
the passage of time
measured in black ink

At a park on Via di Capaccio, Florence.
6 May 1498.

I walked on the rim
in endless circles
over and over
until I stumbled
and fell

well down
in
to the sinners' well.
Cerulean frost,
the bitter water
of separation.

I floundered and screamed
but no one heard me.
I looked up and saw
the circle of sky
change from blue to black
but there were no stars
to offer me hope.
No sound to lift me.
Just bitter water,
dark separation
from He who made light.

Frankfurt am Main.
20 Oct 2011.

In Full Knowledge

If you were born in 1861,
you are most certainly dead.
The last of you, Alice Stevenson
of Piccadilly, old England,
gave up the ghost August 18, 1973
after five score, twelve years
and thirty-nine days of living.
Queen Victoria was still a young
girl on the morning of July 10, 1861.
Lincoln had nearly four years
of fraternal bloodshed ahead of him
before his last show at the theatre.
At the time Alice breathed her last,
another President faced political
death. From Lincoln to Nixon,
Victoria to Elizabeth II.
Only the ancient trees and a few
sea turtles remember those days
of the eighteen-sixties.
No one is left who fought
in the Great War either. Those
millions who knew the horrors
of the trenches along the Front.
They have moved on to better
meadows; they are free to think.
They have the full knowledge
that is given out in death.

On the River Main. Near Frankfurt.
22 Oct 2001.

Chronos

Chronos came after
original sin.
The two's departure
from Earth's paradise
wound up the great clock
and sprung it to life.
We have been under
its watch ever since.
Aside from hunger
or refreshing drink,
we worry whether
we will have enough
time to get it done,
whatever that means.
We even measure
sex by the minutes.

Time is without weight
but it weighs us down.
Some wear it to bed
as they count the sheep.
Few live without it.
Yet, time marches on.
Once it's gone, it's gone.
Limitless itself,
until the End Times;
finite, though, to us.

Kairos and Chronos:
two times, two meanings.
One gives certain life,
eternity in
Heaven's paradise;
the other, just doubt,
regret, death, and dust.

London, England.
8 Sep 1997.

Keeper of the Great Clock

Tonight I was bored
so I climbed up the tower
and talked to Big Ben.
I sat on his minute hand,
not far from the internet,
that small, wireless box
with the flashing red light.
Yes, I sat between analog
history and the digital future,
and not far from the Thames,
where Shakespeare drank
and cursed his muse.
Mere minutes from where
the Queen now sits and sips
her rare brand of emerald tea.
It was the quarter hour,
and my seat was level.
Soon, though, I will find the pull
of gravity sliding me back
to earth, to common reality,
but for these few minutes,
I revel in this space of time
and the familiar quarter notes
of the Cambridge chime.

9 Clagarnach

(CLOY-GER-NACH)

the sound of heavy rain
on the roof.

Frankfurt am Main.
16 Oct 2001.

the seven surprises

Almost everyone loves surprises.
They come both little and small
grand and tall, no notice at all.
Both ordinary and extraordinary
and unique to every one of us.
But they are not at all universal.

Those, I call the Seven Surprises
that unfold in the course of a life.
They are the true breath-stoppers,
the ones that knock us to the ground
or lift us to unquestioned height.

Mortality is the first and perhaps
most unsettling. The realization
that your body is no stronger than
the velveteen rabbit that gets loved
to death, the hard truth that your
days are not only numbered but
also unknown to anyone but God.
It is the first dry butterfly we find
in our barefoot days, not the grey
hairs, that bumps the young mind.

Gravity is the second, the hard jolt
to your bottom as you discover man
cannot fly, that we are tethered like
magnets to this liquid rock. The sin
of envy as we watch the smallest of
birds fly wherever they will, taking
their scenic shortcuts with the crow.

Adversity is the third, a practical
experience with the first squall of life,
the inability to predict the timing
or strength of the storms to come.
The real-world knowledge that life
is not all afternoons of lemon-ade
and Legos, bike rides and late swims
or luck of winning all the marbles.

Inequality, the cousin of adversity,
is the fourth, the ugly truth that not
all are created equal or treated fairly.
We do not walk onto the field
in the same condition or fate.
We do not enter the school of life
with blank slates or unfettered minds.
Silver favours silver; it always has.
The bubbles always rise to the top,
and the short straws are left in the cold.

Sexuality is the fifth, the marvel
and wonderment as we watch our
immature bodies grow and darken,
as we feel the stirrings of intense
stallion pleasure rise to full view,
as we lose ourselves in virgin thrust
and blush, the building, pending
explosive release that is both a shock
and source of pride that first time.
Magnified later in penetrating love.
A gift with power to bless us with life
and some measure of immortality.

Infinity is the sixth and perhaps the most
difficult to comprehend. To imagine that the
finite Earth hangs in a dark box that is
expanding exponentially, and has been doing
so for billions of years. The difficult concept
that there is no end, there is no larger
container that holds the outer space within.

Eternity, the father of infinity, is the Seventh.
The truth that there is One who is omnipresent
from the beginning, omniscient, and omnipotent.
The One who out of His infinite grace and love
for us transforms our mortal souls into eternal
spirits to live with Him in heaven beyond
the bonds of gravity, adversity, and inequality,
leaving the third surprise as the one unknown.

Caisleán sa Garrán. Ireland.
23 Jun 2002.

Rhythmic Feet

I brought up the subject
that the animals are getting smarter
as we ourselves become dimmer
by the day, losing our memories
to the very machines we built.
What we can no longer remember
has crossed over into their world.
The gift from brute to the beast.
They have embraced the idea
that they could someday rule
the world and right the wrongs,
that they could learn to open doors,
to set their fires and capture light,
write their songs in musical notes
and carry a poem on rhythmic feet.

Richmond, Virginia. USA.
23 Sep 1850.

Henry "Box" Brown

In 1849,
in the land of Liberty,
a man once mailed himself
to freedom.

By thinking 'outside the box,'
he put himself inside a box—
a wooden crate three feet
by three feet by two.
One air hole and little room.
Twenty-seven hours by wagon,
train, steamboat, wagon, ferry,
train, and the final wagon.
Two hundred and fifty miles
from Richmond to Philadelphia,
City of Brotherly Love.

I struggle to imagine
how a land considered
so civilised could err
so far from its declared
Conception,
with its puberty not much better

Considered 'dry goods,'
no one even noticed
the man in the box,
or the millions he left
behind.

Ponte Vecchio bridge, Forence.
6 May 1498.

verum scientificum

It is truth,
verum scientificum,
common knowledge
that at any given
moment half the world
sits in the dark,
at the far end of the well
without lamp or fire.

Dawn and dusk,
they are the fringes
of the same coat,
from the same mad
dog that's been chasing
its tail half-way

around the world
since the beginning
of time when

the cave walls were
devoid of crayon
stick art of deer
and hunting men.

Da Vinci said
the sun never saw
a shadow.
Another smart
Southpaw.
True enough.
But the brain
is a source of light,
and there are
plenty of shadows within.
Knowledge and ignorance
are not that far apart;
the width of a crack
separates the genius
from the insane.
Synapses of sanity
that so easily mis-fire.

Central Park. New York City.
21 Apr 1998.

The Rainbow Coalition

Jap Chink Mick
Nip Dink Spick
Wop Pink Frog

Mockie Moke
Limey Kike
Redneck Mammy
Wetback Moonie

Paddy Pong
Yellowfish Wong
Cracker Kraut
Cambo Laut

Camel-jammer
Lugan Greaser
Yid and Goy
Buck and Boy

Oreo Spade
Banana Slope

Colored Ginney
Dago Honkey
Hunkie Rok
Raghead Wok

Jigaboo
Darky Poo
White Trash Nip
the Nigra's Nigger

Herring Choker
Dino Joker
Look, WASP, Gook

small words

mean a little,
Say a lot.

10 Uisce báistí

(ISH-KAH BAWSH-SHTEE)

rain water.

Vienna, Austria.
26 Aug 1920.

Freudian Slip

The old boy
rows
the left boat
out beyond
the
outer bank
As he pulls
the old bay
cups
the bottom
but
rejects the
oar
made of wood
that once lined
the
now-naked
shore
like
so many
men-of-war

Kent, England.
6 May 1958.

Waiting for Rain

She rocks on the porch waiting for the rain
to bless the pansies and the hydrangeas.
It has been a long day of quiet drought.
The earth is parchment waiting for the pen,
but where is the hope in a clear blue sky?
In the morning she hid in the springhouse
where she kept her feet in the cold water
as she struggled with the daily crossword.
Life was a puzzle for the dear woman.
Her husband left the farm for another;
left her without child or a heavy hand
to harvest the farm she had known since birth.
She has spent twenty years alone at nights,
two stale decades of regret and longing.
Even the bi-polar cat would not stay;
not enough milk in the cow could keep her.
Tall trees would get up and go if they could.
Same for the pansies and forget-me-nots,
and now even the rain keeps its distance.
She has a tattered house and battered barn
and a picket gate that never opens.
The storm, it will come in the evening;
it is something she tells herself each day
as she rocks on the porch waiting for rain.

Bruges, Belgium.
3 Jul 1989.

A note to the poet in me:

On good authority

I heard it on good authority
that cicadas are dead in poetry.
Can the cricket be not far behind?
Cold rain still splits the hot tin roof
as the cat laps up the saucer of milk.
Off-page, the trio of church mice
sleep tight in the belfry's height,
right below the inverted bats
hung above the quiet bells at
old St Martins-in-the-fields.
The outside fields, they are green
with lines of sounding rhyme,
where metre and feet converge.
Spring lovers lay on chequered cloth
and while away the bluebird's day.
Oh, to be a young poet again,
when cicadas were still a novelty.

Grafton House, Islesworth. England.
11 Oct 1911.

Indelible Memory

Words born in ink
Sequestered on paper
Sealed in wax
Carried by hand

Received
Opened
Read
Embraced
...Or Rejected
Saved
...Or Burned

Paper, ink, wax, and hand—
four tangibles that carry
five qualities of humanity—
thought and voice;
privacy and intimacy;
and indelible memory

Grafton House. Isleworth. England.
12 Jan 1894.

We Emilys of the World

The world is full of Emily Dickinsons,
poets living in obscurity,
never knowing if their work
will remain hidden until their death,
only then to be discovered and celebrated.
It is spare comfort to know
that I am not alone in this position.
It is the eternal struggle of the artist:
to hone the craft for the Art itself,
countered by the human desire
for others to see what you have made.
It is the subtle nuance of pride and ego
while we wrestle with the sad, cold
reality that, for the vast majority of us,
death will bring the certain ceasing
of our life-work. For all time. Never
to be seen or understood. Ever.

11 Slán

(Slawn)

farewell. go in good health.

Park near the Florence Cathedral.
9 Aug 1498.

short life

Once,
he crawled along the green shoots
seeing the earth up close,
so amused with jungle life.

Then,
he flew above the lush grass
drinking the juice of blooms
so enthused by open heights.

Now,
he fades upon the dry rock
leaving his life of ease,
fast abused by summer's length.

The Academy. Florence.
May 1498.

debits on the left
credits on the right
equal goats and sheep

addebiti a sinistra
crediti a destra
proprio come capre e pecore

Piazza della Signoria, Mid-morning
Friday, 23 May 1498

At the public hanging and burning of Father Savanola of *Bonfire of the Vanities* fame.

ashes to ashes
burned bones to light dust
remnants of a life

Château de Cloux, France.
Twilight. 2 May 1519.

we leave in our eve
as others live in their morn
new memories fade

Château Amboise, France. Leonardo's gravesite.
2 May 1719.

headboard of granite
thick blanket of summer grass
canopy of stars

Edinburgh Castle, Scotland.
4 Feb 1959.

Mind over Matter

The mind is so much
faster than the hand,
and the letters get backed up
somewhere in the bone
between shoulder and wrist.
Like paratroopers
seeing the light of day
they leap onto the page
while a few cower in the wings.
Sometimes a thought skips a beat
and those words are lost forever.
But we gloss over them
and barely notice their absence.
They are the little words of life
Between 'The' and 'End.'

Galway, Ireland
17 Nov 2016.

knackered

I am tired of this world,
something we are not supposed
to say aloud or in print,
at least not in good company.
I know that, but it is true
nonetheless. Scary true.

I would rather live
behind the cerulean curtain,
where the realm is spiritual,
not physical,
where hate has no place;
where we breathe only
oxygenated joy;
where we fly, not walk;
praise, not criticise;
raise, not lower.

We live in a darker world,
where light is limited
to the cracks in the sky.
These are the days after Elija,
and the days that followed Elisha.
We are in the midst of the wilderness,
the nights of lions and tigers and bears,
with a pack of wolves thrown in
for good measure

Index of Poems (Alphabetical)

About the Poet: Peer Lumijnfroost

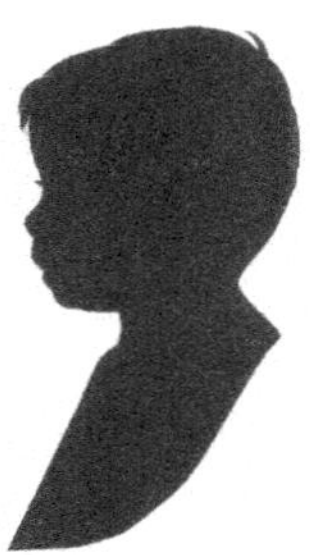

At the age of sixteen Peer Lumijnfroost ("Lumijn") entered the rigorous *la prima accademia di contabilità di Firenze* as a junior accounting apprentice under the direction of Fr. Luca Pacioli. He completed his *praktikum* at the House of de' Medici (*Tuscan Profumeria*). In 1498, on a chance encounter on the Ponte Vecchio bridge, Peer met and began a life-long friendship with the artist Leonardo da Vinci. Leonardo later became his patron and introduced him to the previously unknown Half-Life (*Realm Dimidium*). Over the next five hundred plus years Peer has lived and documented the rise and fall, twists and turns of Western civilisation, while writing poems along the way.

A Tree Never Leaves before the Snow Falls is a treasury of poems included in the author's daily journal he began in May 1498 and continues to this day. Each poem has been thoughtfully translated into modern English from the original language of that day (Lumijn is fluent in 17 different languages and dialects). The sometimes coarse language reflects the human condition as he experienced it.

In 2001, while on a pilgrimage to his native Florence, Lumijn met his kindred spirit, an art student from Frankfurt am Main. He and Tule were married on May 23, 2002 in Dublin, Ireland. Together, they have five children and live at Castle Grove Estate near Tullamore in the Republic of Ireland with their centuries-old friends, *The Marquess and Marchioness of the Irish Midlands.*

Once a season, Lumijn travels to the United States to spend time with his publisher and good friends in the Blue Ridge Mountains near Blacksburg, Virginia.

www.ingramcontent.com/pod-product-compliance
Lightning Source LLC
Chambersburg PA
CBHW020914090426
42736CB00008B/632